Saimunur Rahman

Introduction to E-Commerce Technology in Business

GRIN Verlag

Bibliografische Information der Deutschen Nationalbibliothek:

Die Deutsche Bibliothek verzeichnet diese Publikation in der Deutschen National-bibliografie; detaillierte bibliografische Daten sind im Internet über http://dnb.d-nb.de/ abrufbar.

Imprint:

Copyright © 2014 GRIN Verlag GmbH
Druck und Bindung: Books on Demand GmbH, Norderstedt Germany
ISBN: 978-3-656-74552-5

This book at GRIN:

http://www.grin.com/en/e-book/280494/introduction-to-e-commerce-technology-in-business

GRIN - Your knowledge has value

Der GRIN Verlag publiziert seit 1998 wissenschaftliche Arbeiten von Studenten, Hochschullehrern und anderen Akademikern als eBook und gedrucktes Buch. Die Verlagswebsite www.grin.com ist die ideale Plattform zur Veröffentlichung von Hausarbeiten, Abschlussarbeiten, wissenschaftlichen Aufsätzen, Dissertationen und Fachbüchern.

Visit us on the internet:

http://www.grin.com/

http://www.facebook.com/grincom

http://www.twitter.com/grin_com

1.0   E-Commerce (Electronic Commerce)

Electronic commerce, commonly known as E-commerce or e-commerce, is trading in products or services conducted via computer networks such as the Internet. Electronic commerce draws on technologies such as mobile commerce, electronic funds transfer, supply chain management, Internet marketing, online transaction processing, electronic data interchange (EDI), inventory management systems, and automated data collection systems. Modern electronic commerce typically uses the World Wide Web at least at one point in the transaction's life-cycle, although it may encompass a wider range of technologies such as e-mail, mobile devices, social media, and telephones as well.

Electronic commerce is generally considered to be the sales aspect of e-business. It also consists of the exchange of data to facilitate the financing and payment aspects of business transactions. This is an effective and efficient way of communicating within an organization and one of the most effective and useful ways of conducting business. It is a Market entry strategy where the company may or may not have a physical presence.

2.0   E-Business

E-Business is the term used to describe the information systems and applications that support and drive business processes, most often using web technologies.

E-Business allows companies to link their internal and external processes more efficiently and effectively, and work more closely with suppliers and partners to better satisfy the needs and expectations of their customers, leading to improvements in overall business performance.

While a website is one of the most common implementations, E-Business is much more than just a web presence. There are a vast array of internet technologies all designed to help businesses work smarter not harder. Think about collaboration tools, mobile and wireless technology, Customer Relationship Management and social media to name a few.

3.0   E-Commerce and E-Business

The terms 'e-commerce' and 'e-business' are often used interchangeably but what do these words really mean?

E-commerce refers to online transactions - buying and selling of goods and/or services over the Internet.

E-business covers online transactions, but also extends to all Internet based interactions with business partners, suppliers and customers such as: selling direct to consumers, manufacturers and suppliers; monitoring and exchanging information; auctioning surplus inventory; and collaborative product design. These online interactions are aimed at improving or transforming business processes and efficiency.

4.0   E-Commerce under different perspective

There are several ways of looking at e-commerce which is given below:

Communication: It is the ability to deliver products, services, information, or payments via networks like the internet.

Interface: E-commerce means information and transaction exchange: (Business to business, Business to consumer, Consumer to consumer, and business to government.)

Business process: E-Commerce means activities that support commerce electronically by networked connections. For Example business processes like manufacturing and inventory etc.

Online: E commerce is an electronic environment that allows sellers to buy and sell products, services, and information on the internet. The Products may be physical like Cars, Computers, Books or services like news or consulting.

Structure: Ecommerce deals with various media: data, text, video, web pages, and internet telephony.

Market: E-commerce is a worldwide network. A local store can open a web storefront and find the world at doorstep- customers, suppliers, competitors, and payments services, Of course, an advertising presence is essential.

5.0   Architectural Framework of E-Commerce

Architectural framework of e-commerce means the synthesizing of various existing resources like DBMS, data repository, computer languages, software agent-based transactions, monitors or communication protocols to facilitate the integration of data and software for better applications.

The architectural framework for e-commerce consists of six layers of functionality or services as follows:

1. Application services.
2. Brokerage services, data or transaction management.
3. Interface and support layers.
4. Secure messaging, security and electronic document interchange.
5. Middleware and structured document interchange, and
6. Network infrastructure and the basic communication services.

5.1   Application services

In the application layer services of e-commerce, it is decided that what type of e-commerce application is going to be implemented. There are three types of distinguished e-commerce applications i.e., consumer to business application, business-to-business application and intra-organizational application.

5.2   Information Brokerage and Management Layer

This layer is rapidly becoming necessary in dealing with the voluminous amounts of information on the networks. This layer works as an intermediary who provides service integration between customers and information providers, given some constraint such as low price, fast services or profit maximization for a client. For example, a person wants to go to USA from Bangladesh. The person checks the sites of various airlines for the low-price ticket with the best available service. For this he must know the URLs of all the sites. Secondly, to search the services and the best prices, he also has to feed the details of the journey again and again on different sites. If there is a site that can work as information broker and can arrange the ticket as per the need of the person, it will save the lot of time and efforts of the person. This is just one example of how information brokerages can add value.

Another aspect of the brokerage function is the support for data management and traditional transaction services. Brokerages may provide tools to accomplish more sophisticated, time-delayed updates or future-compensating transactions.

5.3   Interface and Support Services

The third layer of the architectural framework is interface layer. This layer provides interface for e-commerce applications. Interactive catalogs and directory support services are the examples of this layer.

Interactive catalogs are the customized interface to customer applications such as home shopping. Interactive catalogs are very similar to the paper-based catalog. The only difference between the interactive catalog and paper-based catalog is that the first one has the additional features such as use of graphics and video to make the advertising more attractive.

Directory services have the functions necessary for information search and access. The directories attempt to organize the enormous amount of information and transactions generated to facilitate e-commerce.

The main difference between the interactive catalogs and directory services is that the interactive catalogs deal with people while directory support services interact directly with software applications.

5.4   Secure Messaging Layer

In any business, electronic messaging is an important issue. The commonly used messaging systems like phone, fax and courier services have certain problems like in the case of phone if the phone line is dead or somehow the number is wrong, you are not able to deliver the urgent messages. In the case of courier service, if you want to deliver the messages instantly, it is not possible as it will take some time depending on the distance between the source and destination places. The solution for such type of problems is electronic messaging services like e-mail, enhanced fax and EDI.

The electronic messaging has changed the way the business operates. The major advantage of the electronic messaging is the ability to access the right information at the right time across diverse work groups.

The main constraints of the electronic messaging are security, privacy, and confidentiality through data encryption and authentication techniques.

5.5   Middleware services

The enormous growth of networks, client server technology and all other forms of communicating between/among unlike platforms is the reason for the invention of middleware services. The middleware services are used to integrate the diversified software programs and make them talk to one another.

5.6   Network Infrastructure

We know that the effective and efficient linkage between the customer and the supplier is a precondition for e-commerce. For this a network infrastructure is required. The early models for networked computers were the local and long distance telephone companies. The telephone company lines were used for the connection among the computers. As soon as the computer connection was established, the data traveled along that single path. Telephone company switching equipment (both mechanical and computerized) selected specific telephone lines, or circuits, that were connected to create the single path between the caller and the receiver. This centrally-controlled, single-connection model is known as circuit switching.

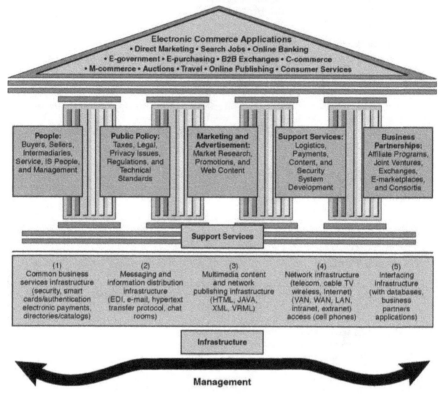

Figure: A Generalized Architectural Framework of E-Commerce

6.0 Classification of E-Commerce Applications

The classification of e-commerce applications is given below:

6.1 Electronic Market

Electronic Market: is a place where online shoppers and buyers meet. E-market handles business transaction including bank-to-bank money transfer also. In e-market, the business center is not a physical building. But it is a network-based location where business activities occur. In e-market, the participants like buyers, sellers and transaction handler are not only one different locations but even they do not know each other.

6.2 Inter Organizational Information System (IOS)

An IOS is a unified system with several business partners. A typical IOS will include a company and its supplier and customers. Through IOS buyers and sellers arrange routine business transactions. Information is exchanged over communication network using specific formats. So, there is no need for telephone calls, papers, documents or correspondence.

Types of IOS is given below:

- **EDI (Electronic Data Interchange)**: It provide secure B2B connection over value added network(Van's)
- **Extranet:** which provide secure B2B connection over internet.
- **EFT (Electronic Fund Transfer):** Electronic Fund Transfer from one account to another.
- **Electronic Forms**: Online (web-pages) forms on internet.
- **Shared Data Base:** information stored in repositories (collection of data) shared by trading partners
- **Supply Chain Management:** Co-operation between company and its suppliers and customers regarding demand forecasting, inventory management and order fulfillment.

7.0 Types of E-Commerce

E-commerce conducted between businesses differs from that carried out between a business and its consumers. There are five generally accepted types of e-commerce:

- Business to Business (B2B)
- Business to Consumer (B2C)
- Consumer to Business (C2B)
- Consumer to Consumer (C2C)
- Business to Government (B2G)

7.1 Business to Business (B2B)

Business to Business or B2B refers to e-commerce activities between businesses. An e-commerce company can be dealing with suppliers or distributors or agents. These transactions are usually carried out through Electronic Data Interchange or EDI. In general, B2Bs require higher security needs than B2Cs. For example, manufacturers and wholesalers are B2B companies.

With the help of B2B e-commerce, companies are able to improve the efficiency of several common business functions, including supplier management, inventory management and payment management.

Using e-commerce enabled business applications, companies are able to better control their supplier costs by reducing PO (purchase order) processing costs and cycle times. This has the added benefit of being able to process more POs at a lesser cost in the same amount of time. E-commerce technology can also serve to shorten the order-ship-bill cycle of inventory management by linking business partners together with the company to provide faster data access. Businesses can improve their inventory auditing capabilities by tracking order shipments electronically, which results in reduced inventory levels and improves upon the ability of the company to provide "just-in-time" service.

This e-commerce technology is also being used to improve the efficiency of managing payments between a business and its partners and distributors. By processing payments electronically, companies are able to lower the number of clerical errors and increase the speed of processing invoices, which results in lowered transaction fees.

7.2   Business to Customer (B2C)

Business to Customer or B2C refers to e-commerce activities that are focused on consumers rather than on businesses. For instance, a book retailer would be a B2C company such as Amazon.com and other companies that follow a merchant model or brokerage business models. Other examples could also be purchasing services from an insurance company, conducting online banking and employing travel services.

7.3   Customer to Business (C2B)

Customer to Business or C2B refers to e-commerce activities, which use reverse pricing models where the customer determines the prices of the product or services. In this case, the focus shifts from selling to buying. There is an increased emphasis on customer empowerment.

In this type of e-commerce, consumers get a choice of a wide variety of commodities and services, along with the opportunity to specify the range of prices they can afford or are willing to pay for a particular item, service or commodity. As a result, it reduces the bargaining time, increases the flexibility and creates ease at the point of sale for both the merchant and the consumer.

7.4   Customer to Customer (C2C)

Customer to Customer or C2C refers to e-commerce activities, which use an auction style model. This model consists of a person-to-person transaction that completely excludes businesses from the equation. Customers are also a part of the business and C2C enables customers to directly deal with each other. An example of this is peer auction giant, Ebay.

7.5   Business to Government (B2G)

It is a new trend in e-commerce. This type of e-commerce is used by the government departments to directly reach to the citizens by setting-up the websites. These websites have government policies, rules and regulations related to the respective departments. Any citizen may interact with these websites to know the various details. This helps the people to know the facts without going to the respective departments. This also saves time of the employees as well as the citizens. The concept of Smart City has been evolved from B2G e-commerce.

8.0   The Benefits of E-Commerce

Few innovations in human history encompass as many potential benefits as E-Commerce does. The global nature of the technology, low cost, opportunity to reach hundreds of millions of people, interactive nature, variety of possibilities, and resourcefulness and growth of the supporting infrastructure (especially the web) result in many potential benefits to organizations, individuals, and society. These benefits are just starting to materialize, but they will increase significantly as E-Commerce expands. It is not surprising that some maintain that the E-Commerce revolution is just 'as pro- found as the change that came with the industrial revolution.

8.1 Benefits to Organizations

The benefits to organizations are as follows:

- Electronic commerce expands the market place to national and international market with minimal capital outlay, a company can easily and quickly locate more customers, the best suppliers, and the most suitable business partners worldwide.
- Electronic commerce decreases the cost of creating, processing, distributing, storing, and retrieving paper-based information. For example, by introducing an electronic procurement system, companies can cut the purchasing administrative costs by as much as 85 percent.
- Ability for creating highly specialized businesses. For example, dog toys which can be purchased only in pet shops or department and discounts stores in the physical world are sold now in a specialized www.dogtoys.com (also see www.cattoys.com).
- Electronic commerce allows reduced inventories and overhead by facilitating "pull" type supply chain management. In a pull-type system the process starts from customer orders and uses just-in-time manufacturing.
- The pull-type processing enables expensive customization of products and services which provides competitive advantage to its implementers.
- Electronic commerce reduces the time between the outlay of capital and the receipt of products and services.
- Electronic commerce initiates business processes reengineering projects By changing processes, productivity of salespeople, knowledge workers, and administrators can increase by 100 percent or more.
- Electronic commerce lowers telecommunication cost the internet is much cheaper than value added networks.
- Other benefits include improved image, improved customer service, new found business partners, simplified processes, compressed cycle and delivery time, increased productivity, eliminating paper, expediting access to information, reduced transportation costs, and increased flexibility.

8.2 Benefits to Consumers

The benefits of E-Commerce to consumers are as follows:

- Electronic commerce enables customers to shop or do other transactions 24 hours a day, all year round, from almost any location.
- Electronic commerce provides customer with more choices; they can select from many vendors and from many more products.
- Electronic commerce frequently provides customers with less expensive products and services by allowing them to shop in many places and conduct quick comparisons.
- In some cases, especially with digitized products, E-Commerce allows quick delivery.
- Customers can receive relevant and detailed information in seconds, rather than days or weeks.
- Electronic commerce makes it possible to participate ate in virtual auctions.

- Electronic commerce allow customers to interact with other customers in electronic communities and exchange ideas as well as compare experiences.
- E-commerce facilitates competition, which results in substantial discounts.

8.3 Benefits to Society

The benefits of E-Commerce to society are as follows:

- Electronic commerce enables more individuals to work at home and to do less traveling for shopping, resulting in less traffic on the roads and lower air pollution.
- Electronic commerce allows some merchandise to be sold at lowest prices, so less affluent people can buy more and increase their standard of living.
- Electronic commerce enables people in third world countries and rural areas to enjoy products and services that otherwise are not available to them.
- Electronic commerce facilitates delivery of public services, such as health care, education, and distribution of government social services at a reduced cost and/or improved quality. Health care services, e.g., can reach patients in rural areas.

9.0 The Limitations of E-Commerce

The limitations of E-Commerce can be grouped into two categories which are:

- Technical limitations and
- Non-technical limitations

9.1 Technical Limitations of E-Commerce

The technical limitations of E-Commerce are as follows:

- There is a lack of s stem security, reliability, standards and communication protocols.
- There is insufficient telecommunication bandwidth.
- The software e development tools are still evolving and changing rapidly.
- It is difficult to integrate the Internet and E-Commerce software with some existing applications and databases.
- Vendors may need special Web servers and other infrastructures in addition to the network servers.
- Some E-Commerce software might not fit with some hardware or may be incompatible with some operating systems or other components.
- As time passes, these limitations will lessen or be overcome; appropriate planning can minimize their impact.

9.2 Non-technical Limitations

Of the many non-technical limitations that slow the spread of E-Commerce, the following are the major ones:

Lack of Awareness: Lack of awareness of the technology and its potential benefits are also equally responsible for the poor growth of e-commerce. Lack of interest and willingness to make a paradigm shift has become a crucial issue. Many companies are not willing to accept that their businesses need a revolutionary change to subsist in the potentially digital world. The single most important challenge today pertains to increasing awareness of the benefits of e-commerce to potential customers, educate the market and the customers will themselves opt for these services.

Lack of Infrastructure: E-commerce infrastructure development is at its infancy stage in Bangladesh. This unsatisfactory development is yet another major bottleneck for successful net business in Bangladesh. This high cost of infrastructure development for e-business is also including the cost of leased lines.

Lack of Confidence: The people in Bangladesh still show hesitancy in buying through the Net. Lack of quality products, timely delivery of products as some of them tend to go out of stock, lack of solutions security are the potential reasons for not developing e-commerce. People do not understand this new way of buying and selling products, i.e. the services in a digital environment which are available online.

Skeptic Attitude: Though the Internet is continuing to grow at a rapid rate, along with e- commerce transactions, the shoppers are still skeptical about safety and have not been quick to trust sending personal information such as credit card numbers or address over the Net. Lack of adequate imagination and understanding of what web-based technologies can do to markets and competition only adds to the delay in economic development. The old business habits are demanding and controlling the business. The risk adverse attitude of the people is conspicuous and waiting for others to lead is also another attitude.

Credit Cards Frauds: In Bangladesh, distribution channels are just one part of the problem related to e-payments. The bigger problem is that of security. All credit cards related transactions are approved offline and given the high incidence of frauds, the banks are extremely wary of approving them. In-fact, there are some unconfirmed reports of a multi-national bank refusing to approve credit card transactions carried out by a large Bangladesh portal.

Absence of Tax Laws: E-commerce over the Net has effectively eliminated national borders. This has posed an important question as to tax on the transactions over the internet. Net business posed many peculiar technological and legal problems making it difficult to impose tax and formulate a sound taxation policy.

Cyber Laws: Another important problem is lack of comprehensive cyber laws so as to ensure safety and protection. There should not be any legal regulations, or barriers to faster and increased development of e-commerce. The crying need of the hour is urgent action to be taken by the Government to enact cyber laws including electronic fund transfer, and amendments of official Secrets Act.

Stock Dilemma: Many people are not too happy with e-commerce trends. Though online shopping may be growing but so is frustration with it. A key source of dissatisfaction is the out of stock dilemma. In most cases, advertised products or services are not available. The options of feedback and not receiving suggestions are also reasons for annoyance. Many online consumers want more detailed information on their purchases but are not available. The Net is becoming more mainstream and the expectations are also becoming more mainstream.

Lack of Skills and Expertise: Lack of skilled and trained personnel impedes the growth of implementation of IT related e-commerce. The use of the Net for trade requires a complex introduction of servers, browser software and knowledge of web design, hosting, promotion and many more skills. It requires understanding many new things. Many Bangladeshi businesses are not prepared to approach electronic commerce. For many business houses for which commerce over internet may not work, would take a lot of efforts for every little return.

Internet Outrage: Failures in networks and the Net itself can play havoc. We read of frequent press reports of internet outrages. The IT industry is notyet attempting to improve network reliability to prevent these outrages. Reliability is a major issue in net business that needs to be attended.

Absence of Cyber Brand Image: Another problem is that advertising and the Net tends to focus on e-commerce rather than on brands found in the real world. This would prove to be a deterrent in ensuring consumer loyalty. The biggest thing going for it is a brand image and power. Though the already existing name is known and trusted, the issue is how to extend it into the new cyber reality. A concern should be to preserve the old values of trust and dependability of the brand, and at the same time, keep it upon on the Net. At the same time, the whole business structure will have to undergo a change re-engineered.

Inadequate Government Role: The government is not taking a serious view of e-commerce related information technology in terms of its promotion. Spreading awareness, imparting education, of the benefits of e-commerce, enacting new cyber laws, amendments to existing commercial laws, developing strong, communication infrastructure are the key domestic roles for the government to play.

No Encouragement from Business Community: The business community is extremely an important sector to be targeted for the introduction of any technological innovations in business. It means it is the business community that sustains e-commerce and greatly influences the thinking and adoption process of various segments of the society to move forward in the field of information technology. It motivates the people who share the courage and conviction to move the new business paradigm.

Preferring Foreign Sites: Online shoppers in Bangladesh do not prefer Bangladeshi websites to a large extent and prefer US and other foreign websites. There are many reasons for this as they provide better selection, prices, stock, quality products, shipping, payment process security, customer service and wide variety of sites among other things.

Difficulty of Reengineering: The web business structure will have to undergo a drastic change and be reengineered. It is not just about having a website or about sticking a web address on conventional advertising or transferring a few people to a new division and designation. It is about breaking free and creating new web services to satisfy the existing customers.

Internet for Small Business: Another problem is that for major project, a large consumer product company needs profiling of customers who undertake transaction through e-commerce. E-commerce is still being dominated by large corporations. Small and medium sized business houses have to take advantage of everything on the Net. Online shopping is clearly catching on with consumers and retailers need to keep pace with growing demands.

Infant Stages: Electronic commerce is still in its infant stage. Bangladeshi commerce is establishing itself in the area of internet business. The concept of e-commerce is still in evolutionary stage, it is a job that still needs to be defined. The IT function has not grown beyond the marketing department and credit cards, merchant accounts, digital signatures and prompt payment and one has to realize that the e-commerce role is more about harnessing technological resources to deliver profits to the Net users. Only a few Bangladeshi big houses have gone online to explore the potentials of e-commerce.

E-commerce has yet to take off in Bangladesh, because Bangladeshi consumers are wary of leaving their re credit card numbers on the Net. They eye the neighborhood shopkeeper with suspicion and drive a hard bargain. So, e-commerce websites are losing thousands of customers.

10.0   Electronic payment

Electronic payments are either debit or credit payments that are processed entirely electronically, with the value passing from one bank account to another bank account. Credit payments, often referred to as Electronic Credit Transfers (ECT) or Electronic Funds Transfers (EFT), are where a customer instructs their bank to make a payment, electronically, to another bank account. Debit payments, known as direct debits, are where a customer instructs their bank to allow the payment to be charged to their bank account.

11.0   Advantages of Electronic payment

Electronic payment systems are software systems that enable online credit card processing. Via an electronic payment system, users can browse an online catalog and purchase items online through automated online transactions. Launching an e-commerce website ultimately improves the way of doing business, increases level of sales, expands business to local and foreign markets and improves relationships with existing customers.

11.1   Sales

Your online presence creates a stronger company profile and yields access to new local and foreign markets. The increased availability of your products to a larger customer base via an electronic payment system extends your current mail-order services, and reaches other potential customers and local businesses through increased exposure. An online catalog, with online ordering and payment functions, to sell your products provides the added benefit that you can display information about each item for sale and indicate whether it is available from stock. Displaying related products on the pages viewed is also a subtle sales promotion that might induce the customer to purchase more products.

11.2   Customer Support

Electronic payment systems enable faster order processing and delivery, which caters for higher efficiency in both business to business (B2B) and business to consumer (B2C) models. Improved customer support services, shorter lead times, and a twenty-four-hour service around the globe ensure a satisfactory shopping experience for your customers. Via the electronic payment system it is easy to implement a personalized service for your customers by enabling subscription services and provide timely information about special offers and promotions. Newsletters are an effective marketing strategy that entices your customers to return to your website and purchase more products.

11.3   Improved Marketing

An e-commerce website will assist your business in gaining competitive advantage and heightening public interest. An online presence will not only improve and facilitate your current marketing strategy but it will also yield new opportunities in the business to business environment through increased exposure and increased efficiency.

11.4   Running Costs

An electronic payment system introduces potential cost savings through an improved business model and effective supply chain management, since much of the transaction process will be automated. Whereas, in a manual system your clients need to first contact your company to obtain a quote and check for product availability, through an electronic payment system, they can check your price offers, delivery times and place their orders in a couple of minutes. Lower running costs and shorter lead times enable the company to cater for bulk orders received from local businesses.

12.0 Disadvantages of Electronic payment

12.1 Online Security

When we check out at a merchant and use our credit cards we must present photo ID. However when making online payments there is no real authentication process to verify that the person entering the information online is not a criminal. Without this verification process time becomes of the essence when it comes critical to dispute a fraudulent charge made using your credit/debit card because research is needed to prove your case.

12.2 Missed Errors

Can you imagine being in business since 1970, each time you needed to replenish inventory you contacted your supplier with whom you have a personal relationship to place your order. The supplier delivers your goods in a timely fashion. Upon delivery an invoice is provided and you either pay COD (cash on delivery) or mail in your payment. Now 21st Century technology is presented; you submit your order online which requires payment before delivery. Once the goods arrive you realize you mistakenly order the wrong material. Now you have you merchandise that cannot be used and you are out your money. More time is now needed to return the "unnecessary material" to wait for the replacement order to arrive. For many people the old way was more efficient.

12.3 Fees

Management courses have taught us that there is an opportunity cost for every choice we make. Surprisingly, OPS are no different. Since the core business of many organizations is not IT based and more specifically not specialized in Online Payment Systems an outside vendor is required to provide the online payment services. An Online Payment Systems vendor like PayPal requires the merchant to pay a convenience fee ranging between 2.2%-3.9%. Would it be beneficial to use their services as opposed to alternative payment methods? For corporate organizations this fee may prove to be inconsequential. However, for the small business owner these fees could equate to astronomical figures eating away at the bottom line.

And also many more.

13.0 Typical E-Payment Types in E-Commerce

The modes of payment have surely changed in so many different ways. But it is important to take note that this change is on a positive note and not a negative one. In relation on how we get to make payments, the introduction of payment systems into the market has clearly made things a lot better. These systems are designed to make money transfer from one account to the other quick and easy as it can be done in a matter of seconds. The systems will come in two distinct features but for now we want to take a quick look at some of the different types of electronic payment systems. These are the kind of systems that will accept payments through electronic means.

13.1 Electronic cards

Electronic cards are designed to reflect your bank account. By having one, it means that you definitely do not need to visit your bank physically in order to access your account. Mostly cut out of hard plastic material to make them durable, the cards will have a magnet trip that allows the machines to be able to gain access to your bank account electronically. They will come in three major types. The debit card, the credit card and the prepaid card. All that the vender has to do is to swap your card across the payment system where a message will be sent to your bank and immediately reply with a confirmation message. All this is done in a matter of seconds.

13.2 Internet

This is a unique payment system that allows transactions to occur online. There are normally different sites through which you can be able to do this but the two most commonly practiced methods of online payments are direct transfers from one bank account to another or the use of cards.

13.3 Use of mobile phones

Mobile phones are turning out to be more than just a communication gadget. They are even referred to as smart phones due to the many additional features that they have. Although it will give you limited transactions to carry out, the best kinds of payment system available for mobile phones are mobile banks. There are a number of mobile subscriber firms that have developed the app that allows the mobile users to have an account that they can gain access to through their mobile phone number.

13.4 Online accounts

This kind of payment system is slowly on the rise. We can attribute this to the increase of online shopping. Having an online account with either PayPal money bookers and or any provider allows you to be able to transfer funds more quickly as there are no restrictions and limitations on what you can do with your electronic money. One can be able to access their online accounts through their phones and or computers. These accounts are so simple to use.

14.0 The ICDT Business Strategy Model

The ICDT model, developed by Albert Angehrn at INSEAD, is a systematic approach to the analysis and classification of business-related Internet strategies. It serves as a basis for identifying how existing goods and services can be extended and redesigned to take advantage of the Internet, as well as suggesting the characteristics of new goods and services made possible through this new medium.

Angehrn's model is based on four virtual spaces:

14.1 Virtual Information Space

This space is where a firm displays information about their organization about their products or services. This space is the easiest space for the business to enter and it is a typically first step taken towards the virtual market space.

For example E-commerce major concerns are

1. The information that it displays is accurate and current.
2. The information that it displays is only viewed by authorized users.
3. Customers can easily find the site and negotiate through it once they have reached the site.
4. The site accessible without long unit times.

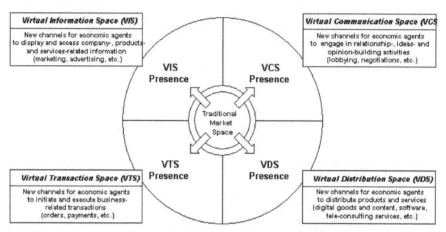

Figure: *ICDT Business Strategy Model*

14.2 Virtual Distribution Space

This space is used to deliver the product or services required or purchased by the consumer. For virtual delivery to occur, the products being delivered must be digital (software) or the service performed digitally (ex – online broker). Online news services and software companies have been quick to market and deliver their products electronically.

For e-Commerce major concerns are

1. Delivery of products and services to legitimate customers only.
2. Reliable delivery of product and services

14.3 Virtual Transaction Space

This space is used to initiate and execute the sales order which are nothing but transactions. Apart from those companies engage in virtual distribution space, most companies have been reluctant to enter this space. The major concern contributing to this reluctant is data security.

The major concerns of E-commerce are

1. Security over data.
2. Accuracy and integrity of processing data methods.
3. Privacy concerns by customers.

14.4 Virtual Communication Space

This space is used to enable relationships building, negotiations and exchange of ideas such as char room, virtual communities, forums etc. E-commerce is effected if such a community is a service for which its members pay.

15.0 Mobile Commerce

Mobile e-commerce (m-commerce) is a term that describes online sales transactions that use wireless electronic devices such as hand-held computers, mobile phones or laptops. These wireless devices interact with computer networks that have the ability to conduct online merchandise purchases. Any type of cash exchange is referred to as an e-commerce transaction. Mobile e-commerce is just one of the many subsets of electronic commerce.

Mobile e-commerce may also be known as mobile commerce.

16.0 Why M-Commerce Concept is Became So Popular

The M-Commerce Concept is Became So Popular because of the reasons described below:

16.1 Affordability of mobile devices

It is no denying fact that mobile devices like cellphones and tablets are far more affordable than desktops and laptops, and an average Bangladeshi consumer doesn't have much disposable income in his hand to buy high end devices. Plus, one doesn't even really need expensive smartphones to shop online or make mobile transactions.

16.2 Doing things on the go

Mobile devices give the freedom to do things like shopping, booking tickets, making hotel reservations etc. anytime anywhere. And in Bangladesh, there is a large young consumer base, who want fast instantaneous processes on the move. One doesn't need to wait to reach home or to a cyber cafe to pay bills or make an urgent purchase online.

16.3 Mobile Internet connectivity

M-Commerce customers are not bound by limited wired and Wi-Fi Internet connections. In the last 3-4 years, the number of users who access the Internet through a 3G connection has grown to round 22 Mn. Now compare this with the 15 Mn fixed line broadband connections accrued over the last 17 years, there is a notable difference. Even though E-Commerce has spread its roots throughout the country, it still hasn't reached the places where people have no broadband or no computer. M-Commerce could and will change this.

16.4 Mobile Payments

Mobile Payments is a new mode of payment as an alternative to traditional methods like cash, cheque credit cards etc. A customer can use a mobile phone to transfer money or to pay for goods and services. A mobile payment could be made by an app, data connection, IVR and even SMS, so anyone who has a bank account can make a transaction. This could aid in reducing cash-dependencies of people, particularly in rural Bangladesh.

16.5 Security

Mobile platforms are still relatively free from viruses and other threats. And even in case of a fraudulent activity, credit tracking by GSM/GPRS/GPS is easy and quick. Thus increasing the credibility, and giving better assurance to the skeptical Bangladesh population. Also, seldom do people part from their phones, so there are less chances of misuse of login information that may happen on computer systems.

16.6 Bridging the gap between E-Commerce and conventional stores

Brick and mortar stores are getting a lot of heat from online stores, which are luring their customers away by offering better product prices and discounts. When a person goes out for shopping, mobile acts as a conduit between the two poles, people compare prices online before buying something. This could be, and is being used by retailers to their benefit by offering location based services, barcode scanning, and push notifications to improve the customer experience of shopping in physical stores.

16.7 Greater target audience for advertisements

The problem with online advertising is that people have to be 'online' to view it. Several E-Commerce players in India have come out with TV commercials to advertise their websites. However, mobile is a better platform to do the same. Even with Government's regulation on bulk messaging, companies could still target a mass of people collectively by sending promotional content via SMS if a user hasn't activated the DND service or wants to receive those ads.

16.8 Low tariffs-High revenue

Mobile data tariffs in Bangladesh are the cheapest in the world. Unlike PC Internet affordability of 3G connectivity has improved significantly. For instance, Airtel reported its 3G price to be BDT 0.60 per MB last month, which is less than the global average of 3 cents or BDT 3.49. Such low rates will encourage people to use more of Mobile Internet, and eventually engage into M-Commerce as well. Considering the large mobile user base in Bangladesh, the government could work with mobile companies to increase the overall revenue, by increasing Average revenue per user (ARPU).

16.9 Personalization

In a true sense Personal Computers are not really personal. Desktops and even laptops are shared by multiple people living in the same family or working together in an office. However the same isn't true in case of cellphones. Whichever strata of the society a person may belong to, a phone has become an indispensable extension of oneself. People are more comfortable using their phones for various activities, as it gives them a sense of privacy and security, while offering easy usability. Since already there are way more mobiles in Bangladesh than computers, M-Commerce could gradually grow bigger than E-Commerce.

17.0 M-Commerce Application

Many more people have access to a mobile phone that to a computers and this means that m-commerce has the opportunity to connect not just big businesses but also small business and consumers on a massive scale. In this sense, mobile phones have the potential to bridge the digital divide and allow organizations and individuals to reach out to one another more easily than ever before.

After the appearances of a new technology a remarkable growth occurs in it. This has been the same in mobile commerce.

Mobile Commerce has gained increasing acceptance amongst various sections society in last few years. The reasons for its growth can be traced back to technological and demographical developments that have influenced many aspects of the socio-cultural behavior in today's world. Mobile services have registered impressive growth in preceding years and m-commerce is slowly but surely showing signs of a healthy growth.

The major mobile commerce applications along with details of each is given below:

17.1 Travel and Ticketing

By utilizing the B CODE technology or NFC technology we could use the mobile phone as a means receiving E-Tickets. B CODE tech consists of sending text SMS which is scan able from the mobile phone display screen through the related set. So by receiving the chosen SMS, the ticket is practically received and we could present the mobile phone to the scanning machine at the ticket receipt spot.

17.2 Commerce

Commerce is the exchange or buying and selling of commodities on a large scale involving transportation of goods from place to place. It is boosted by the convenience and ubiquity conveyed by mobile commerce technology. There are many examples showing how mobile commerce helps commerce. For example, consumers can buy products from a vending machine or pay a parking fee by using their cellular phones, and mobile users can check their bank accounts and perform account balance transfers without needing to go to a bank.

17.3 Education

Similar to other wired technologies, mobile wireless technologies have first been used in industry sectors such as business. The movement of mobile wireless technologies in education is a recent trend, and it is now becoming the hottest technology in higher education.

17.4 Enterprise Resource Planning (ERP)

In the coming mobile commerce era, users will want to be able to have access to the right resources and work as efficiently as possible– whether they are traveling, seeing a customer or working at other remote locations– with their ERP systems. Many ERP vendors are currently researching for means to provide mobility to ERP users. They attempt to connect employees to their work more effectively than ever before by enabling mobile phones and other wireless devices to become a new kind of tool to seamlessly exchange information, automate data entry and perform a range of transactions anytime, anywhere

17.5 Entertainment

Entertainment has always played a crucial role in Internet applications and is probably the most popular application for the younger generation. Mobile commerce makes it possible to download game/image/music/video files at anytime and anywhere, and it also makes on-line games and gambling much easier to access and play. It is projected that by 2005, 80 percent of all mobile users in the United States and Western Europe will play mobile games at least occasionally.

17.6 Health Care

The cost of health care is high and mobile commerce can help to reduce it. By using the technology of mobile commerce, physicians and nurses can remotely access and update patient records immediately, a function which has often incurred a considerable delay in the past. This improves efficiency and productivity, reduces administrative overheads, and enhances overall service quality. Mobile technologies such as PDAs, Laptops or Tablet PCs can be of great value in hospitals and healthcare facilities by allowing better access to critical information – e.g. patient status, staff and patient location and facilities availability. Healthcare facilities that choose to adopt such technologies may be able to not only perform better but ultimately provide more efficient and better quality of care for patients.

17.7 Inventory Tracking and Dispatching

Just-in-time delivery is critical for the success of today's businesses. Mobile commerce allows a business to keep track of its mobile inventory and make time-definite deliveries, thus improving customer service, reducing inventory, and enhancing a company's competitive edge. Major delivery services such as UPS and FedEx have already applied these technologies to their business operations worldwide with great success.

17.8 Traffic

Traffic is the movement of vehicles or pedestrians through an area or along a route. The passengers in the vehicles and the pedestrians are all mobile objects, ideal clients of mobile commerce. Also, traffic control is usually a major headache for many metropolitan areas. Using the technology of mobile commerce can easily improve the flow of traffic in many ways. For example, a mobile handheld device can have the capabilities of a GPS, such as determining the driver's exact position, giving directions, and advising on the current status of traffic in the area. A traffic control center could also monitor and control the traffic according to the signals sent from mobile devices in the vehicles.

18.0 Limitations of M-Commerce

Despite the fact that the use of M-Commerce is growing rapidly there are still limitation that causes limited use of M-Commerce:

18.1 Bandwidth

The limited bandwidth that can be support by mobile devices currently is very small which causes web developers to reduce the usage of rich data.

18.2 Screens Size

The screen size of a mobile device is very limited. This also limits the viewing capacity of the user.

18.3 Less Powerful Processors

Due to the slow processing speed web developer would have to use server side scripting which will bring more load to the servers.

18.4 Cost of Wireless Connection

As wireless connection of a mobile device to the internet is still a relatively new technology the cost of using such connection is also expensive as the technology is still under heavy development.

18.5 Lack of Security

Currently there is no dedicated standard protocol for M-Commerce which is a very big limitation.

18.6 Lack of Standard

There are a lot of device operating systems and platforms, middleware solutions and networks and make application development for the wireless Internet a formidable task with compare to the wired operating systems. Currently there is no standard dedicated for the M-Commerce Applications. Currently several progress/efforts is going on for this.

18.7 Health Limitation

Cellar mobile frequencies is sometimes dangerous to health. Sometimes they are cause of Cancer. It is invented that they sometime interfere the operations of some medical devices i.e. pacemaker.

19.0 Mobile Generations

G in 2G, 3G and 4G stands for the "Generation" of the mobile network. Today, mobile operators have started offering 4G services in the country. A higher number before the 'G' means more power to send out and receive more information and therefore the ability to achieve a higher efficiency through the wireless network.

As the name would suggest, 1G was the first generation of mobile networks. Here basically, radio signals were transmitted in 'Analogue' form and expectedly, one was not able to do much other than sending text messaging and making calls. But the biggest disadvantage, however came in the form of limited network availability, as in the network was available only within the country.

2G networks on the other hand, were based on narrow band digital networks. Signals were transmitted in the digital format and this dramatically improved the quality of calls and also reduced the complexity of data transmission. The other advantage of the 2G network came in the form of Semi Global Roaming System, which enabled the connectivity all over the world.

Between 2G and 3G there was a short phase in between where mobile phones became sleeker and more 'pocketable' if we can call it that. This is popularly referred to as 2.5G where the quantity of radio waves to be transmitted was much lower. This in turn had an effect on the shape and structure of mobile phones. But most of all, 2.5G helped in the ushering of GPRS (General Pocket Radio Service).

The 3rd generation of mobile networks has become popular largely thanks to the ability of users to access the Internet over devices like mobiles and tablets. The speed of data transmission on a 3G network ranges between 384KBPS to 2MBPS. This means a 3G network actually allows for more data transmission and therefore the network enables voice and video calling, file transmission, internet surfing, online TV, view high definition videos, play games and much more. 3G is the best option for users who need to always stay connected to Internet.

4th Generation mobile networks are believed to provide many value added features. In addition to all the 3G facilities, data transmission is believed to go through the roof with speeds ranging between 100MBPs to 1GBPS. Phew! Happy talking, surfing, conferencing, chatting, networking, partying, or whatever you want to do on your mobile phone.

Table 1: Comparison of *1G-4G* Technologies

Technology / Features	1G	2G	2.5G	3G	4G
Start/ Deployment	1970/ 1984	1980/ 1991	1985/ 1999	1990/ 2002	2000/ 2006
Data Bandwidth	1.9 kbps	14.4 kbps	14.4 kbps	2 Mbps	200 Mbps
Standards	AMPS	TDMA, CDMA, GSM	GPRS, EDGE, 1xRTT	WCDMA, CDMA-2000	Single unified standard
Technology	Analog cellular technology	Digital cellular technology	Digital cellular technology	Broad bandwidth CDMA, IP technology	Unified IP and seamless combination of broadband, LAN/WAN/PAN and WLAN
Service	Mobile telephony (voice)	Digital voice, short messaging	Higher capacity, packetized data	Integrated high quality audio, video and data	Dynamic information access, wearable devices
Multiplexing	FDMA	TDMA, CDMA	TDMA, CDMA	CDMA	CDMA
Switching	Circuit	Circuit	Circuit for access network & air interface; Packet for core network and data	Packet except circuit for air interface	All packet
Core Network	PSTN	PSTN	PSTN and Packet network	Packet network	Internet
Handoff	Horizontal	Horizontal	Horizontal	Horizontal	Horizontal and Vertical

-- The End --

www.ingramcontent.com/pod-product-compliance
Lightning Source LLC
La Vergne TN
LVHW042317060326
832902LV00010B/1562